George Bird Grinnell

Boise State University Western Writers Series   Number 122

George Bird Grinnell

By Ley Eva

Connecticut College

Editors: James H. Maguire
John P. O'Grady

Business Manager:
James E. Hadden

Cover Design and Illustration
by Arny Skov, Copyright 1996

Boise State University, Boise, Idaho

Copyright 1996
by the
Boise State University Western Writers Series

ALL RIGHTS RESERVED

Library of Congress Card No. 96-84310

International Standard Book No. 0-88430-122-2

Printed in the United States of America by
Boise State University Printing and Graphic Services
Boise, Idaho

George Bird Grinnell

I

As the United States frontier moved west in the nineteenth century, it developed as a locus for the myth of the American superman, a fabled combination of self-reliance and self-development in which the frontiersman fought savage beasts and wild Indians to push a great civilization through plains and forests to the Pacific Ocean. Ironically, to participate in the frontier's expansion was to contribute to its destruction: as destiny and technology seemed to carry the nation toward its grand fulfillment, the wilderness with its challenging animals and murderous savages diminished. By the 1880s, thoughtful Americans believed that the West could no longer provide the character-building battlefield as it was known to Daniel Boone, Davy Crockett, or pioneer women on the Oregon Trail. As the United States reached its geographical limits and its position as an industrial power after the Civil War, the need seemed to arise for a supportive mythic vision, one that would encourage not only the preservation of wilderness values but also their use in justifying America's development into an empire-building society. As an American myth, the frontier ethos would provide continued revitalization of the nation, keeping it from degenerating into "soft" European or "feminized" ways, as Theodore Roosevelt called them.

Not coincidentally, this sense of the western frontier as spiritual and moral necessity paralleled cultural interest in recording and studying this natural world and its creatures before they vanished and were no longer available for inspiration or the challenge of renewal. Efforts to preserve the wilderness, if only in books and museums, grew after the Civil War. Americans collected and catalogued everything from trees and glaciers to prehistoric bones and Indian relics, scholarly tasks that correlated with establishment of national parks and forests, and with a passion for writing and reading about American natural history. Displacement of Indian tribes onto reservations represented a kind of collecting, allowing access to a large if diminishing population of "Stone Age" peoples who had been part of the frontier struggle but were now available, however unwillingly, for study by historians and ethnologists. The common element supporting this interest in collecting dinosaur bones or native language systems was the sense of establishing a specifically American mythos, a guide to what made the country "great." For many students of the West, the crucial concern was to show that vital moral qualities—courage, self-reliance, integrity—as well as more physical aspects like endurance, could serve a post-frontier world.

Preservation of the vitalizing myth often required that its historians and scholars be participants in this demanding life, not just armchair observers. The period's most famous example would be Theodore Roosevelt, who by 1900 had established himself as spokesman for both hunting nature and preserving it and also for an essentially nostalgic view of the frontier as the source of American virtues, which he summed up in terms like "manliness" and his concept of "the strenuous life." Roosevelt actively participated in this myth-making by living ranch life in Dakota, collecting bird skins and big-game trophies, and writing histories of his hunting adventures, books which describe the importance of physical struggle in making a man a "man." In works like *Ranch Life and the Hunting Trail* (1888) he presented a self-experienced frontier vision which required that wild animals and frontiersmen be worthy of their wilderness: leading "wild, free, reckless lives . . . frank, bold, and self-reliant . . . the hunter is the arch-type of freedom" (82-83). "Nostalgic" because admiring of a basically unrecoverable past, Roosevelt was following in the footsteps of historians of the American West such as Francis Parkman. This sort of "contact" history—Parkman had traveled on the Plains himself before writing *The Oregon Trail* (1849)—went along with a romantic view of heroic and violent men civilizing the wilderness while keeping alive manly virtues deriving from that conflict. Jackson Lears calls this late nineteenth-century ideal "distrust" of modern industrial society, a distrust that found expression in "primitivist veneration for vitality" and "nostalgia for an innocent society" (146). Men like Roosevelt believed the frontier had provided society with a source of moral rejuvenation.

George Bird Grinnell, a contemporary and friend of Roosevelt, was one of the most influential historians and preservers of the West. Nine years older (1849-1938) than Roosevelt, Grinnell was available for this late frontier kind of myth-making; he too turned himself into a "frontiersman." Like Roosevelt, Grinnell came from an Eastern Establishment family; his father was broker, or "agent," for Cornelius Vanderbilt, financier of the Union Pacific railroad and its western expansion. He grew up in a large Victorian house in what is now upper Manhattan, but was once part of the estate of the naturalist, John James Audubon. His earliest schooling was with Audubon's widow, who lived next door. He began his own career as a naturalist in the time-honored way: hunting and collecting bird and animal skins, just as Audubon had done in preparing models for his paintings in *The Birds of America*.

Grinnell went to Yale in 1866, becoming interested in paleontology, a "new" science under the direction of Professor Othniel C. Marsh, with whom he went on his first "old-fashioned bone hunt" as he called it, in the western plains in 1870, an adventure in exploration and research on the frontier that changed his life. Or, rather, turned it into that many-faceted life lived in both East and West which makes Grinnell typical of his class and period.

When he came back from the Marsh expedition, his father put him into the family brokerage firm, a job Grinnell disliked; however, he continued to work in paleontology with Marsh at Yale. After an 1872 hunting trip with the scout Luther North, he served as naturalist on Custer's 1874 Black Hills gold-seeking expedition and on a survey of the Yellowstone region in 1875. In 1874 he dissolved the family firm, which had nearly "gone under" with the 1873 market panic, brought on in part through speculation on Western railroad shares. Grinnell continued research at Yale, where he was awarded the Ph.D. in paleontology in 1880, writing his dissertation on that quintessentially Western bird, the roadrunner. What this early history suggests is that he was becoming that combination of businessman and naturalist, hunter and preservationist, typical of Eastern-based "frontiersmen" from his model, Audubon, to his friend Theodore Roosevelt. It was a time when "innocence" and "vitality" seemed to be running out.

Grinnell carried on this double life by successfully managing various family properties, the exception being a ranch in Wyoming, which was not as profitable an operation. The proof of his powers, however, lies in his editorship of the influential sports and nature journal *Forest and Stream* (later, *Field and Stream*), for which he began to write in 1873, serving as its editor and publisher from 1880 to 1911. He used the journal in part as a public platform to press for conservation of wildlife, development of the National Parks System, and creation of a public attitude favoring preservation of wilderness. At the same time, his interest in that other frontier phenomenon, the Plains Indian, led him into efforts to preserve those vanishing cultures through collecting the tribes' stories and histories. His interest in the Pawnees, Blackfeet, and Cheyennes led to his becoming overseer of the Blackfeet on their Montana reservation and to publishing his definitive two-volume study of the Cheyennes in 1923, the work for which he is best known as an anthropologist.

Grinnell is, in consequence, an important representative figure in American culture of the late nineteenth century. As a member of the Eastern financial world, his money derived, however indirectly, from exploitation of the frontier he watched vanish under the force of United States expansion. At the same time, he often expressed distaste for the Gilded Age society for whom he wrote. His nature essays and his journal, *Forest and Stream*, appealed to a new middle-class audience which could accept the transformation not only of subsistence hunting into sports hunting but of the grizzly bear and antelope into subjects for the tourist and nature writer's camera and pen. There is, however, an element here of what might be called "elitist democracy" in Grinnell's continuing nostalgia for a simpler and freer heroic past when the frontier established a natural "upper class" in its hunters and scouts.

It can also be argued that collecting hunting trophies, prehistoric bones, and soon-to-be-lost Indian ceremonies are all part of an archivist's regret for what is passing away. One example of this American ambivalence about the past is the founding by Grinnell and Roosevelt of the Boone and Crockett Club in 1887. Designed to further "manly sport with the rifle," but also to advance the cause of game preservation and the animals' natural histories (*American Big Game Hunting* 9), the club accepted as members the Eastern power elite: bankers, congressmen, and the military, many of whom owned ranches in the West or had investments there.

The club was named for those two widely admired early frontiersmen, "renowned in every quarter of the Union for their skill as game-hunters, Indian-fighters, and wilderness explorers." Boone and Crockett, nevertheless were "types of the pioneer settlers" to be equated with "the bridge-builders, the road-makers, the forest-fellers . . . who laid the foundations of this great commonwealth" (*American Big Game Hunting* 319-20). This admiration for brutal and often destructive superheroes is the club's contribution to the myth of the frontier as a vital source of "manly" values. Their exclusively male spectral presences continued to justify hunting and living like Indians. These were tests of endurance and self-reliance for men who spent most of their days running the nation from their desks, not their horses.

Grinnell hunted and "lived hard" his entire adult life; he wrote or edited a number of works on hunting, from Charles Hallock's *The Sportsman's Gazetteer and General Guide* (1877) to *American Game-Bird Shooting* (1910). He was that paradoxical American, a hunter of game on the frontier and a recorder of its decline. He lamented the destruction of the buffalo—and of the people, Indian and white, who lived off them. Grinnell plays an important role not only as a mediator between the wilderness and its evolution into American myth but also as a popularizer of our present images of the frontier, the frontiersmen, and the Plains Indians.

II

Grinnell's major writing is found in his nature essays, with which he initiated his career and which appeared throughout his life; his collections of American Indian stories and myths; his biography of frontier scouts and of important Indian leaders, most of which is incorporated in his anthropology of Plains Indian tribes; and his children's fiction. He is famous, of course, as an influential environmentalist, and in his many years as editor of *Forest and Stream*, he produced numerous essays defending or promoting conservationist causes, from protection for wildlife in Yellowstone

National Park to securing passage of the Lacey Migratory Birds Act to establishing Glacier National Park with his own eponymous glacier. His writings in this regard are often political in intent; the best of them, however, are based on personal observation and represent a significant development of that important European-American genre, the nature essay.

The clue to Grinnell's writing lies in his successful use of narrative to create a sense of presence, that quality David Levin calls "the illusion of participation" (14-19): storytelling which conveys the intensity of closely observed personal experience. While his writing is carefully researched when necessary, more importantly, it is based on Grinnell's own involvement. Sometimes this means recounting a grouse hunt; at other times it means writing a history of Indian warfare based on his knowing the informants personally. Often he had ridden over the battlefield many years later with aged combatants. His first major essays derive directly from his youthful experience, one in which nature follows romantic literary convention: the initiation of the innocent, classically educated, Eastern "dude" into frontier life and its dangers. For this twenty-one-year-old Yalie, the trip into Nebraska and Wyoming with Marsh in 1870 as a "bone-hunter" was formative. There Grinnell was exposed to his lifetime subject matter: big game; Stone Age cultures; and famous scouts like Buffalo Bill Cody, heroes about to "domesticate" into sideshows and fiction.

Grinnell claimed his only knowledge of the West up until this trip had come from the novels of Mayne Reid, a writer of popular romances whose extravagant heroes enjoyed adventures more fantastic than those of Parkman's history or James Fenimore Cooper's fiction. On the practical side, Grinnell learned to hunt, make camp, and survive from day to day. At one point he and a companion, out looking for game to feed the men, lost their directions, were forced to hide from enemy Sioux, and escaped a prairie fire

(Reiger 31-38). A tenderfoot's adventure, the experience suggested a kind of dramatic and individual heroism not unrelated to events in Reid's or Cooper's fiction.

Although Grinnell provided careful detail and atmosphere in his early essays, his own experience often seems to repeat the romantic conventions of adventure stories. In their elevated language and their descriptions of an impressionable traveler happening upon sublime natural scenes—in this case the Rockies—these essays, written for *Forest and Stream* (1873), are heavily influenced by the nineteenth-century romantic narrative tradition. "Elk Hunting in Nebraska," "A Day with the Sage Grouse," and "The Green River Country" represent the hunter or traveler alone before wilderness grandeur. "The Green River rolls southward an impetuous torrent, its volume constantly increasing as it receives the tribute brought by a thousand channels from the lofty mountains through which it flows." The river's waters are "dark and black as it sweeps through some narrow passage where the sun's rays never penetrate, but assume when spread out in the clear light of day the pale green color from which it takes its name" (Reiger 46).

On the river's banks the observer, like Wordsworth on the banks of the Wye, can imagine distant reaches of the river that are unseen and also can fantasize about wildlife, the "little pine squirrel" gazing "at us with his round, black eyes, wondering, no doubt, what the strange creatures are that invade these mysterious solitudes" (Reiger 49). Where "Nature is the only husbandman and . . . deer and elk the only cattle," the sensitive essayist can speculate about withdrawal into the wilderness, to a "little cabin" for the "sportsman or naturalist" now looking back at that seductive vision from his desk in New York City. Mountains here may be "stern and immutable in their rugged magnificence," as late nineteenth-century landscape painters like Thomas Moran presented them on canvas. The painters' use of contrast between mountains and men participates in a conventional dialectic that Grinnell uses, too, as when he describes campers' white tents "showing bright against the green willows" (Reiger 47).

The "true" citizens of this world are the mountain men who could still be found in the wilderness in 1870: they are praised for being "masters of their own lives." One, Ike Edwards, was also a New Englander in ancestry, like Grinnell, but was known in the West to be "a man of great daring, an excellent hunter, and a most skillful trapper." The mountain men's "mode of life appealed strongly to a young man fond of the open"; the young writer cannot imagine "a more attractive—a happier—life than theirs" (Reiger 45-46). Such romantic nostalgia extends even to a party of men observed around a campfire, "Bearded, bronzed by exposure to all weathers, and clothed in buckskin," who turn out not to be a party of trappers but "members of some scientific expedition," Grinnell's own fellow Yale students.

It is worth noting the conventionality of Grinnell's early nature essays because, like those of John Muir and other contemporaries, they derive from the romantic tradition. But Grinnell had no real interest in Transcendentalism and its later quasi-mystic visions; his writing continues its romantic vein, but hard-driving narration begins to displace nostalgic panegyric. In his 1873 essay describing a buffalo hunt he made with the Pawnees in 1872, he can give us a conventionally rhetorical scene, the sun pushing "aside the rosy curtains of the east" where the "white-headed eagle rears her gigantic brood" and the "prowling Sioux" returns "from some foray upon the luckless settlers" (Reiger 60).

As the essay evolves, however, this florid style is abandoned for a graphic picture of "four thousand Indians on the march": "At the head of the column walked eight men, each carrying a long pole wrapped round with red and blue cloth and fantastically ornamented with feathers, which fluttered in the breeze as they were borne along. These were the buffalo sticks, and [they] were religiously guarded at all times, as the success of the hunt was supposed to depend largely upon the respect shown to them" (Reiger 63). When the essay was prepared for inclusion in Grinnell's 1889 volume on the Pawnees, the detailing is yet more explicit, the sticks becoming "buffalo staves . . . slender spruce poles, like a short lodge-pole, wrapped with blue and red cloth, and elaborately ornamented with bead work, and with the feathers of hawks, and of the war eagle . . . . While borne before the moving column, no one is permitted to cross the line of march in front of them" (Brown 16; *Pawnee Hero Stories* 277-78). This is a small example of Grinnell's effort to make us see the Indians on the move: with children playing games, with women on ponies, children and puppies in their arms, and with many Pawnees walking rather than riding to save their horses for the coming buffalo chase.

Romantic elements remain, the Pawnees happily falling into the type of the Natural Man: "Armed with these ancestral weapons [bows and arrows], they had become once more the simple children of the plains, about to slay the wild cattle that 'Ti-ra'-wa' had given them for food. Here was barbarism. Here was nature" (*Pawnee Hero Stories* 296). Most of the essay, however, is devoted to establishing presence rather than conventional sentiment. The Pawnees find a buffalo cow somehow standing on a cliff-side ledge where it can't be killed. An Indian tries to shoot the cow from above, "but his old arm would not go off. He snapped it half a dozen times, and then, discouraged called out something to us below." Grinnell is to shoot; the cow "responded by shaking her head angrily, and whisking her tail." But suddenly "the cow bent forward and fell on her knees, and the Indian above dropped down on her back" (*Pawnee Hero Stories* 287-88). Grinnell's own "first" buffalo has appropriately "monstrous" size and horns and hoofs "which shine like polished ebony" (Reiger 65); but the chase after it and the path of the bullet are exactly described: " . . . the ball entering near the root of the tail ranges diagonally forward and comes out at the shoulder."

Grinnell increases the sense of immediate participation by shifting to the historical present and the plural first person: "On we go, mile after mile, and still no sign of halting" (Reiger 67). Furthermore, he keeps firm visual control by moving the viewer's eye from the immediate scene to a picturesque general view, the observers riding to a hill to watch the "spectacle" of "Many brown bodies . . . stretched upon the ground, and many more . . . dashing here and there, closely attended by relentless pursuers" (*Pawnee Hero Stories* 301). Grinnell is not only exact in capturing sequential movement, hurrying the eye toward an arresting visual point; he is also careful to locate the action in physical space, the buffalo in their valley, the Pawnees on their bluff.

The romantic perspective is still present, of course, not only in the withdrawal of the eye to a dominant position above the chase but also in a certain sentimental attitude increasingly guarded against but turning up throughout his early work: the feelings associated with seeing the frontier world "vanish" before his eyes: "The scene that we now beheld was such as might have been witnessed here a hundred years ago. It is one that can never be seen again. Here were eight hundred warriors, stark naked, and mounted on naked animals. A strip of rawhide or a lariat, knotted about the lower jaw, was all their horses' furniture. . . . For the moment they had put aside whatever they had learned of civilization" (*Pawnee Hero Stories* 295-96). Grinnell's admiration for physical strength, the hunt for wild animals seen as essential and eternal testing of men, the "savage" nudity of the warriors—all of that required a certain amount of romanticizing to give the Pawnees mythic stature. But his perpetuation of the romantic vision is secondary to his interest in reporting what goes on before his eyes rather than his feelings as reporter.

In the later phases of mountain exploration and description, American writers on nature could develop transcendental longings, as in the case of Grinnell's contemporary, John Muir, whose lyricism looks back to Emerson's essay "Nature" (1836). For example, take this visionary moment in Muir's *Travels in Alaska*: "when we contemplate the whole globe as one great dewdrop, striped and dotted with continents and islands, flying through space with other stars all singing and shining together as one, the whole universe appears as an infinite storm of beauty" (5). Other naturalists such as Ernest Thompson Seton set about domesticating the wilderness metaphorically with books like *The Biography of a Grizzly*, forerunners of the Disney-fication of nature. Grinnell's later writing rarely adds ornamentation and never aspires to flights of symbol reading or anthropomorphizing. His series, "A Trip to North Park" in the Rockies, written for *Forest and Stream* in 1879, presents scenes where an exact sense of presence is heightened by careful use of metaphor, without heightening symbolic readings: ". . . the largest beaver meadow I have ever seen. I presume that there were 500 dams in sight, most of them kept in good repair . . . the whole from the height looked like a silver net spread over an enormous carpet of emerald velvet" (Reiger 136). We have only to compare such a passage with those of more visionary writers like Muir to appreciate Grinnell's restraint.

III

Ironically, Grinnell's initiation into frontier life was part of the opening up and consequent exploitation of the wilderness he enjoyed. His admiration for heroic men like Buffalo Bill Cody and Frank North, whom he equated with "bridge-builders" and "civilizers," may have been sincere, but it would only contribute to the idolizing of figures used to market the West for economic development and tourism. Just as his crusading journal *Forest and*

Stream turned into *Field and Stream*, his own writing represents a domestication of the wilderness for American middle-class consumption. His Indian stories often first appeared in popular journals like *Scribner's,* and his popularizing books on the Indians were part of a wave of sentimental myth-making in the 1890s and later that gave us warrior portraits on calendars and Charles A. Eastman's *Indian Boyhood* (1916) with its acculturated language ("The Indian boy was a prince of the wilderness"), one of many nostalgic accounts of pre-contact life.

Grinnell could write comparable books, like the simplistic *When Buffalo Ran* (1920), a slight novel for children. He could also write *The Indians of Today* (1900), which follows his formula of combining Indian stories and accounts of ceremonies with an overview of Indian society, in this case represented by a brief review of every reservation in the United States, including statistics on tribal populations and Grinnell's commentary on the Indians' success or failure in becoming self-supporting citizens. For all Grinnell's primitivist veneration for "vitality," he very much accepts his contemporaries' view that the Indian had to vanish before civilization's advance, to be transformed into a peaceful farmer or cattle-raiser, educated and tax-paying. In spite of himself, Grinnell inevitably becomes an apologist for the post-conquest Indian. His ethnological studies represent an essentially tragic picture of the extermination of one culture by another and its replacement by the fictional Red Man.

Grinnell's feelings about this process are ambivalent. He records a conversation with a Pawnee chief on the poverty-stricken Oklahoma reservation when he was collecting myths and stories for his first major anthropological venture, *Pawnee Hero Stories and Folk Tales* (1889). He tells the chief he intends to record life from the "olden times to put all these things down in a book, so that in the years to come, after the tribe have all become like white people, the old things of the Pawnees shall not be forgotten." The chief repeats, in agreement, that this is a good thing, "so that our children, when they are like the white people, can know what were their fathers' ways" (vi). In some sense, Grinnell's ethnology represents a perverse national epic in its memorialization of an heroic past no longer available to its own people save in a form transcribed by another culture.

Grinnell's views of the Indian do not change much from his earliest studies. His writing about them does change, however, as the "prowling Sioux" gives way to carefully recorded confrontations with Indians Grinnell had come to know closely. Early on he established an approach which he believed represented a "truer" view of Indians than that represented by Helen Hunt Jackson's *Ramona* (1884), a novel which is "charming" but has too much "romance" and "coloring" to provide an objective record of Indian life (*Blackfoot Lodge Tales* xii-xiii). Grinnell's aim is "truth" and a picture of the "Indian mind" given by the Indian himself.

In his introduction to *Blackfoot Lodge Tales: The Story of a Prairie People* (1892), Grinnell lays claim to a certain originality in using stories and myths—imaginative material—as introduction to the "real" Indian, "the true, natural man" (xi). As he has recorded them, his Pawnee and Blackfeet tales show "pictures of Indian life drawn by Indian artists . . . from the Indian's point of view." Furthermore, "there is nothing about them of the white man"; he has taken the stories down "as they have been told to me by the Indians themselves, not elaborating nor adding to them . . . as nearly as it is possible to render those words into the simplest every-day English" (xi, xiii). Hence a more "unusual" and "scientific" account than that of other researchers (letter 29 July 1889).

In some sense what Grinnell does is nothing new. Henry Schoolcraft in the 1830s relied heavily on stories and myths in his massive study of the Iroquois. H. M. Loomis had done the same for the Micmac and others in his 1884 *The Algonquin Legends of New England*. The new journals in ethnology and folklore were filled with such material. Grinnell is, however, claiming that his collections are closer to what informants actually said and are more "true" because the Indian is telling his own story. This insistence on the absence of a mediating white "author" is a fiction which Grinnell wanted to believe promised authenticity, another romantic ideal close to his wish to achieve the effect of narrative presence. Everything we know about the necessities of translation, however, has to raise the question of how much Grinnell was involved in telling the story.

Grinnell's basic anthropological mode is narrative: storytelling with its attention to location, detail, sequence. Authenticity is the aim here, and such a style correlates with his ambivalent view of his subject: the "Indian mind." He repeats this view in several works: the Indian is like "his white brother" save that he is "undeveloped"; intelligent but with "the mind and feelings of a child" (*Pawnee Tales* xii). He is "barbarous" and "savage," without self-control, believing that "war is the noblest of pursuits" (xv). Furthermore, the Indian does not conceptualize; he is a "close observer" who cannot reason beyond his familiar world, "because he has no knowledge on which reasoning may be based" (*Indians of Today* 22-23). Narrative comes naturally to Grinnell and it could be argued that it might seem the closest stylistic equivalent to the way Indians think, as Grinnell understood it: locally, in particulars.

He may also mean his anthropology is "true" or "scientific" because he does not leave out anything that might offend white readers; some of the sentiments the Indian expresses "may horrify your civilized mind, but they are not unlike those which your own small boy might utter" for "blood and wounds and death . . . used to be a part of the Indian's daily life . . ." (*Blackfoot Lodge Tales* xi). Related to this point is another, a response to the ideal of the Indian as "natural man." Grinnell is concerned to show that Indians possess a moral code, a conscience, a sense of guilt—qualities which earlier writers like Colonel John Dodge denied, treating the Plains Indians as savages without integrity or a sense of communal morality. Grinnell's close studies of his subjects, especially of the Cheyennes, reveal how intricate, if necessarily unconceptualized, tribal laws of right and wrong could be. Though he uses terms like "barbarous" and "savage," they derive in part from the once-popular categories set up by the early ethnologist Lewis H. Morgan, but they are modified by Grinnell's many years of observation of Plains life.

Grinnell's anthropology, in both form and content, is thus founded on narrative, on myth and story representing the "Indian mind." His first book combining narratives and their cultural context, *Pawnee Hero Stories and Folk Tales* (1889), has the subtitle, "With Notes on the Origins, Customs and Characters of the Pawnee People." His second, *Blackfoot Lodge Tales* (1892), is "The Story of a Prairie People." This approach becomes formulaic: each book opens with a collection of stories and closes with an account of the tribe's prehistory, social and cultural life, and a review of its present condition. The Pawnee volume includes a chapter by John Dunbar on the Pawnee language. In contrast to those earlier books, *The Punishment of the Stingy and Other Indian Stories* (1901), a collection of tales from several tribes, has no anthropological discussion. Beginning in 1915, Grinnell returns to his earlier pattern, however, in his organization of Cheyenne material.

The Pawnee narratives are divided into "hero tales" and "folk tales." By the first category, Grinnell seems to mean historical events and characters that have been incorporated into the Pawnee mythos and that therefore tell us what Pawnees think about and how they do so. For instance, the opening "tales" establish a pattern for defining the hero and heroism. Evidently about people who once lived, the first two tales are about young men who set off on war parties to steal horses but end up becoming emissaries for peace between tribes. In "Comanche Chief, the Peace-Maker," a young Pawnee on an honor-winning raid, falls in love with a Comanche girl. After a long search for her family, he lies down in her tepee, forcing her family and finally the entire camp to accept him as her husband, though he came as an enemy.

Grinnell must have seen "Comanche Chief" as a typifying story for teller and audience: the hero is brave and committed to his passion, challenging customs to win the girl. Trickery delighted Indian audiences, and the young man tricks the Comanches into accepting him, not only by getting into the girl's lodge and laying his blanket over her, but by then wearing her robe while the tribe's old men debate what to do with him. Her grandfather decides, after smoking the council pipe, "I do not wish to condemn to death a man who is wearing my granddaughter's blanket" (37). The hero has brought presents of things the Comanches have never seen, such as mirrors. The grandfather also wants to eat what the Pawnees have and he has only heard about: corn, beans, and squash. So he has a humorous motive for saving the boy's life. The story illustrates Grinnell's insistence that the Indian is not the dour savage of convention but the possessor of wit and humanity. And a lover of peace: the Pawnees and Comanches "bury the hatchet."

The narrative hinges less on political commentary than upon the boy's disruption of tribal customs and his breaking into the highly ritualized bride-search pattern. As is the case in many stories here, the conclusion is a description of a ceremony designed to recover social equilibrium after this break: following lots of pipe smoking, Comanche Chief becomes something of a culture hero introducing the Comanches to new foods and to peace. The mythic element is aligned with the historical: we learn at the end that the protagonist was a real person, leader of the Ski'-di band of Pawnee, "and a progressive man of modern times" who "sent his children East to school at Carlisle, Pa.," and died on 9 September 1888.

Grinnell's style, for all his argument that he changes or interpolates nothing in the oral original, still suggests editorial modification. Conversations he cannot have heard are reported in detail, as are accounts of journeys and clothing worn. Nor can we expect that narrative from nonliterate speakers should follow so exactly the principles of European-American narrational techniques. Thematically, the story illustrates Grinnell's interest not only in the passion associated with seeking honor or love but also in the community's handling of such disruptive forces.

Another story, "Lone Chief," opens with a mother's advice to her son about how to be a man with integrity, but the principal action derives from the hero's seemingly irrational decision to "give his body to the enemy"; for no explicable reason, the boy, at first known as "Running Chief," does not wish to live any longer. With a friend, he deliberately goes into the enemy Wichita camp, challenging them to respond to his act of bravery. The narrative emphasizes dramatic action as the camp confronts this wild gesture with its appropriate ceremonies for dealing with the stranger. The Wichitas are won over. Their leader tells the two companions, "By your bravery you have saved yourselves. You shall have the road to your home made white before you . . . . You are not a chief, but you are a chief" (61; 63), a witty commendation Grinnell must have enjoyed, as well as the irony in the situation. Food, horses, and honor reward courageous action even if founded in despair. Running Chief receives a new name, "Lone Chief." The camp has accommodated the irrational, and an essential ethical code has been affirmed.

Grinnell also must have liked the "authentic" here; the boys involved are carefully noted to have returned to the Pawnee camp in March 1869. "Authentic" would also apply to the picture of basic human nature, since Grinnell often shows heroes weeping, turning back from a charge on the enemy out of fear, making such irrational decisions, unlike the conventional picture of the stolid Red Man. Furthermore, Grinnell is consistent in never annotating or theorizing about meanings or ethnological interpretations. He insists on the tales carrying their own metaphoric representations of the "Indian mind." It is perhaps this resistance to theory that led Ruth Bunzel to categorize him as a "dedicated amateur" in the developing discipline of anthropology (*Golden Age of Anthropology* 112).

Curiously, Grinnell's collections of Pawnee and Blackfoot material contain a large number of tales with elements of the mysterious and the supernatural. Such tales illustrate man's spiritual relationship with nature or with the "other world," often following closely the folk tale paradigms of nineteenth-century collections like those of the Brothers Grimm. Frequently they are stories of initiation, like the hero stories, depicting the triumph of a youngest boy or girl over inimical human or inhuman forces. "Hansel and Gretel" comes to mind, but so do other European tales where wit or love or patience give the helpless child or victim of injustice power over enemies.

In the Pawnee story, "The Snake Brother," the elder brother breaks a taboo about eating two kinds of meat together—here, buffalo and squirrel—and he shape-changes into a snake. What is important about the tale is that the taboo-breaker becomes a benign force of nature, helping his younger brother in warfare. The younger brother thus brings the snake presents such as horses, scalps, and even a woman whose husband he has killed with this filial power! The violence and the service performed for demonic forces, often underplayed but present in European fairy stories, appear more obviously here but with the same threat to community, unless they are brought into useful social control. In "The Dun Horse," a spirit horse imposes trial tasks on a poverty-stricken boy to whom it also gives power in war. The boy, however, must use the gift only four times; if he tries for five, he will be punished. Of course, the boy does want more; the magic horse dies, only to be reconstituted through the boy's love and his patience and endurance.

Grinnell is clearly interested in the moral and ethical implications of these tales. In the Clatsop "The Punishment of the Stingy," cheating Blue-Jay's family metamorphose into birds and fly away from him. But Grinnell does not belabor the obvious conclusion. Rather, the narrative turns on the protagonist's control of supernatural powers, and his character contributes to the plot's development. Sometimes the mythical element enters into explanations for present-time events. In "Ti-ke-wa-kush" the man with the power to call the buffalo, a familiar lord-of-the-animals topos in myth, saves the tribe from famine. With his death, this power is lost; hence the necessity for hunting as we do today. Grinnell insists on the historical "facts" here: "Big Knife, a Skidi, who died only recently said that the man was alive in his time" (141). It is important to add that Grinnell, true to his thesis of authenticity, never translates speech into the Victorian diction of "thees" and "thous" or the flowery locutions of literary ethnologists like Daniel Brinton attempting to suggest the "otherness" of tribal speech patterns.

In the subsequent *Blackfoot Lodge Tales*, Grinnell provides an enlarged structure with material in three categories. "Stories of Adventure" begins with another account of a chief who wants peace—here, with traditional enemies, the Snakes—and then moves to tales with significant supernatural trappings. In "The

Lost Woman," a strangely tentative spirit helper—"I will try, I think I can"—brings a man's wife, stolen by the Snakes, back to him. This story is balanced by "The Bad Wife," a woman who nearly destroys her husband and his people when she is captured by the Snakes, only to join that tribe and marry another man. We know this wife is evil, not only through her vanity but also because she becomes chief of the Snakes, an obvious perversion of the natural order. As usual, these stories have moral or ethical components illustrating the operation of codes of conduct less refined than those of white society, given the narrower range of Plains Indian experience, as Grinnell would point out, but nevertheless stringently observed.

Sometimes the narrative derives from the simple breaking of a taboo. In a delightful ghost story, "Heavy Collar and the Ghost Woman," a hunter accidentally sleeps near the bones of a dead woman. The ghost pursues her victim with raucous cries—which we have to assume Grinnell has altered from their original sexual nature—driving the frantic man back to camp and to the puzzlement of his people. In an effort to get rid of the ghost, who is about to destroy the people who have crowded into a single tepee in terror, Heavy Collar's mother tries to use her powers against the apparition. In a surprise ending, it kills her and leaves, obviously taking her as a sacrificial substitute for her son. The bizarre events and the humor of the situation echo Japanese ghost stories transcribed by Lafcadio Hearn and popular at the time. The amoral and gratuitous cruelty of such Blackfoot tales only substitutes scalping and torture for the brutality found in folk tales around the world.

In certain early tales, Grinnell does not always write well. An effort to capture direct speech becomes simplistic, sometimes curtailing a more complex examination of motivation. When the hero of "The Peace with the Snakes" decides on death, we are told "His heart was sad. His people and his relations had left him, and he had made up his mind to give his body to the Snakes" (*Blackfoot Lodge Tales* 5). For an adventure story like this, not much more presentation of motive is required. But some of the following details, as when Owl Bear cuts off the braids of the enemy Snake with whom he has spent the night, seem to require a more thorough context. And sometimes dialogue is in short "Indian-speak": "I am the same as you. I am the chief. I like you. You are brave . . ." (6). Some of this kind of thing can be put down to Grinnell's wish for immediacy: "Could he kill him and yet escape?" or "Too late! Too late! Strange that in all that great camp no one should have seen him killed" (65). This represents a theatrical shift in point of view inconsistent in tone. And sometimes the improbable becomes more than that. Grinnell is obviously making up dialogue for effect when in "The Lost Woman" he has a husband and wife, trying to escape from their pursuers, carry on a lengthy discussion of their plight (14-15). Grinnell never writes as awkwardly again.

"Stories of Ancient Times" is mythic history, providing accounts of the origin of important Blackfoot cult objects and practices, such as the medicine pipe and the beaver medicine. It is in the third section of *Blackfoot Lodge Tales* that his effort to equate a story's events with a plain but effective directness of style is best illustrated. "The Blackfoot Genesis," in its narrative simplicity, is a classic re-telling of mythic beginnings. In a world before time began, power could be used for good or evil; however, its use by Old Man is not arbitrary but for the people's survival on earth. Old Man travels toward the north, making the world as we know it, shaping hills and valleys with his body, raising a landmark butte. Like the other parts of his story, that one is true: "there you can see it today." In the prehistoric past, the buffalo had long beards and were armed, killing the people, who could not defend themselves. Old Man shows these first men and women how to make bows and arrows, in typical Grinnell detail. Once they have turned on their animal persecutors, Old Man teaches them how to make fire, for "it is not healthy to eat the raw meat." Then, in a reversal, he describes how bears and buffalo will come as dreamhelpers. He makes other people, and animals yet further north, of clay. Finally it is Old Man who marks off the boundaries of Blackfoot territory, limits enemies must not cross. And the myth comes up into present time: "Our forefathers gave battle to all people who came to cross these lines, and kept them out. Of late years we have let our friends, the white people, come in, and you know the result. We, his children, have failed to obey his laws" (144). How much the understated stylistic directness of the narrative is the consequence of Grinnell's reading in other mythic transcriptions and how much is "unmoderated" story taken down exactly from his informants, we can never know. But here the appearance, at least, of oral tale simplicity is powerfully achieved.

Again, the "lesson" in such myths and tales is that boundaries, obeying long-established customs, ruling individual drives, are important. Divine or human power must be incorporated into the community, or it becomes destructive. In the Blackfoot story "Kutoyis," the warrior of that name lives in egotistical isolation apart from his camp, refuses to help feed his aged in-laws, and must be destroyed by his alter ego, Clot of Blood, who then releases the hidden food supply of buffalo. Newly acquired power must be tamed. Warrior initiates who gain strength through trials are frequently shown sitting alone, unidentified, on a hilltop, until invited back into the camp and passed through cleansing rituals, ceremonies which, in some sense, these stories themselves represent.

Grinnell is showing us imaginatively, rather than through an anthropologist's analysis, how very close to their myths and stories the lives of these people are, their sense of time and causality differing so very much from our own. These are charmed children who once believed in Old Man's story. The second half of both books on Pawnees and Blackfeet is descriptive anthropology growing out of the first half: a detailed record of all that an intelligent outsider can observe of a limited Stone Age world (*Blackfoot Lodge Tales* xv). We get a chapter on what can be known or guessed about tribal prehistory and migration to the Plains, followed by another on daily life in camp, an imaginative vignette of the usual events from sunrise to night. Chapters on social organization, hunting, and warfare are followed by others on tribal religion, important ceremonies, and what Grinnell in the Pawnee volume calls "medicine and mystery." This last is a history of inexplicable healing of illness, of men who are shot dead and yet recover, and of other "magical" things. Such stories are often hearsay but they are also reported sincerely as told by a reliable informant, sometimes not Indian. Grinnell sees this as worthwhile anthropological material which contributes to our sense of the tribe's imaginative world.

Grinnell shares with his contemporary ethnologists a passion for collecting detailed information, but unlike Franz Boas and his students, he is entirely uninterested in theoretical formulations or phonetic transcriptions of tales. As a descriptive anthropologist, he is closer to someone like James Mooney, who also recorded firsthand experience among the Kiowas and Cheyennes. And he is also closer to the nineteenth-century explorers of Africa and the Americas whose personal contact with strange tribes was usually described in a highly metaphoric prose in which the Other was part of an observed landscape being opened up for conquest and economic exploitation. Grinnell would have denied this politicized view of his relation to his informants, in part because of his deep intimacy with many individual tribal members and his expressed concern for tribal welfare over the years. The language of the Pawnee and Blackfoot texts, however, can still edge into the romantic when Grinnell paints generalized pictures of Indian life. The pre-contact period on the Plains is, for him, an Edenic time when the tribes were "happy and cheerful . . . living that wild, free life that was natural to them" (*Blackfoot Lodge Tales* 181), with an unlimited food supply and chances for glory in war and horse-stealing. In this idyllic pastoral vision, men and women in their best costumes danced together "as light faded from the western sky," the women "holding their arms and hands in various graceful positions" (185). Later, with night, "came the rehearsals of the wonderous doings of the gods" with "many a moral for the instruction of youth."

Such description becomes increasingly rare in Grinnell's writing and is never used in describing a tribe's judicial structure or how a tepee is erected. It does remind us, however, that Grinnell brings to his anthropology his view of the Plains as a lost Paradise: Blackfoot society was narrow and violent but it was also deeply moral and religious, one to be admired and its history preserved. Given his background and his view of the wilderness as necessary to American society, Grinnell's scholarly vision is nostalgic, the noble dead on their burial platforms standing in contrast to the surviving tribesmen of 1890, struggling to farm their wretched reservation fields (180). In his study of the Cheyennes, this commemorative style is dropped but not, perhaps, the original ideals that took him into anthropology in the first place.

IV

Certain romantic views of the wilderness do in fact continue in other Grinnell works and certainly extend into his works of biography and popular fiction. Like his Jack Danvers series of boy's books, beginning with *Jack the Young Ranchman* (1899), his biography of Frank and Luther North, *Two Great Scouts and Their Pawnee Battalion* (1928), demonstrates Grinnell's admiration for heroic men and the models, represented by frontiersmen, of moral and stalwart response to the wilderness. Here romantic elements appear less in style than in point of view. Scouts like Buffalo Bill Cody and Frank North, who knew their wilderness and led troops or settlers into it for defense or settlement, were types of Daniel Boone or Davy Crockett. These were "quiet, modest men" who did not know fear, "brave, as in the old war days most men were, because they thought of their work and not of themselves." Grinnell speaks from the heart: "In these old fightings, the men who took part in them were not concerned about what might happen to themselves. . . . They went on from day to day doing only what they had promised to do—fulfilling their agreements." He makes a sad comparison with his contemporaries: "The men of the present day cannot conceive of the risks and the labors involved in that old wild life. They have had no experience to make them understand this" (*Two Great Scouts* 18-19).

As with Theodore Roosevelt, such frontiersmen represent a primitive aristocracy in which moral qualities are identified with the "natural man," not with the intellectual or commercial man. Like Daniel Boone for an earlier American historian such as Bancroft, the scout for Grinnell was not only fearless and responsible, he also had no "material motives" for his work in clearing away the wilderness. When we examine the lives of Boone, however, or of the Norths as Grinnell presents them, we see their stories are filled with violence directed against the Indians. In recording this aggression without comment or with praise for the Norths' fearlessness, Grinnell implicitly condones it. What we see is the "enemy" struggling to hold on to his tribal land and culture, "fightings" that provide the historian with his major subject matter. Grinnell, furthermore, is really interested not in the personality of the elder brother, Frank North, but in his conventional figure as an heroic leader. The great scout is evidence of an historic movement, now over. The older North several times raised a group of Pawnee "scouts" in the last phase of this people's tribal existence. The Pawnees welcomed the chance to fight against their traditional Plains enemies and to serve the United States, which, in spite of all the Pawnees' loyalty, would send them to an Oklahoma reservation. Re-organized several times between 1865 and 1877 as adjunct members of the United States Army, the scouts' purpose was to lead counterattacks against the Sioux, Comanches, and Cheyennes who were raiding settlements and the route through Nebraska on which the Union Pacific railroad was being built. Like other Indian scouts, they accompanied army maneuvers as guides, helping in the destruction of their own culture.

What Grinnell has written in *Two Great Scouts* is a history of a sequence of battles important in opening up central Plains territory for white development. He relied heavily on first-person interviews, especially with the younger brother, Luther, a source the commentator on Grinnell in Howard R. Lamar's *The Reader's Encyclopedia of the American West* (1977) considers unreliable. Grinnell also relies on a detailed battle-by-battle account that reads more like a chronicle than a narrative. His biography is ostensibly anti-romantic: "The wild west pictures of scouts dashing madly off on a gallop for a long ride are not faithful" (231), a comment which precedes a step-by-step description of North surviving a prairie snowstorm. Such description demonstrates Grinnell's belief that there should be true heroism in the circumstantial detail of a life lived quietly but with integrity.

This is nevertheless a romantic vision of a frontier leader given mythic stature. Grinnell establishes a context with descriptions of early encounters with the Pawnee, among them that of Zebulon Pike in 1806, one in which Pike stands up against the Pawnee, who are in far larger numbers. He faces down their chief over flying the United States flag in place of the Spanish: "Except honesty, there is nothing that the primitive Indian respects so much as he respects courage . . ." (43). Later in the century, Frank North has to be seen as a leader carrying on this tradition. The Pike story is quoted from a journal kept by another traveler of the period, and Grinnell has researched the history of the Kansas-Nebraska frontier. While he will frequently let the informant tell his own version of an event, the usual voice is third-person, with detailed accounts of action that could only come from informants equally attuned to detail, from the exact number of scalps taken in a skirmish to the name of a dead Cheyenne (Red Bull).

A good example of this reportorial technique is that describing the death of an embattled Sioux warrior. Grinnell gives the ancestry of the half-breed Pawnee-Spanish scout who killed him: Baptiste Behale, a government interpreter. Behale takes bow and arrows in place of his gun to the field; there he fights with the Sioux, also armed only with bow and arrows. Finally Baptiste shoots the Sioux, running on foot, with an arrow: "It struck him under the right shoulder, went clear through his body and came out low down on the left side. He stopped, took hold of the spike end of the arrow, pulled it through himself, fitted it on to his bow, shot it back at Baptiste, and fell over dead." The victor ducks behind his horse's neck and "the arrow whizzed over his body about two inches too high" (140). Grinnell has obviously taken these details from Behale himself, but the written presentation of the scene, with its sequence of details, could only come from the writer's passion for historical accuracy and the drama such narrative can set up.

In some sense the picture of Frank North suffers from this approach: we never see the man himself save in action. His courage and ability to command in any battle situation is unquestionable.

In scene after scene he rides into the enemy, guns blazing, as Western heroes must do. In an early passage he nearly loses his horse, is almost killed by the Cheyennes who pursue him, runs, shoots, ducks arrows until he and a companion can get back to camp. There they find the Pawnees trying to kill an "old" Cheyenne who, like North, bravely holds out, until North orders a final effort at killing him. Shot dead, "He was at once struck and scalped by the Pawnees" (98-99).

In one of many later episodes, a Sioux "medicine man" whom the Pawnees thought could not be killed, jumps on North's famously swift horse and escapes. In an "incomprehensible sequel," North rides after him, only to see the fleeing Sioux stab a knife into the stolen horse and prepare to defend himself with bow and arrows, where he might have escaped by riding away. North says to his attendant Pawnees, "Now let me show you how much of a medicine man he is, . . ." and gallops toward the Indian, shooting him dead in spite of the enemy's arrows (182). As usual, there is no comment on North's feelings about his horse or the brave if "crazy" Sioux; the action is simply and directly reported as though it carried its own dramatic justification.

This episode is typical of Grinnell's authorial objectivity, a long way from the earlier narrator's involvement in a Pawnee buffalo hunt. This technique of letting the facts "speak for themselves," however, gives us very little of Frank North's inner life, a subject that never very much interests Grinnell, and which a concentration on narrative as adventure story discourages. Such detailing of the facts also becomes implicit commendation of the violence and the killing of "hostiles" in which North, his Pawnees, and the regular military were involved. Grinnell tells the story of a Pawnee named Crooked Hand, a great warrior who, "it was said," had killed "more than one hundred of the enemies of the Pawnee." Grinnell calmly notes that at a scalp dance, Crooked Hand wears a robe ornamented with seventy-one scalps he had taken. He was "quick in action and speech and also quick tempered, but good natured and always full of fun" (133). Such a description gives us a slightly more complex presentation of personality than is usual in *Two Great Scouts*, but the savagery behind Crooked Hand's scalping prowess seems acceptable to Grinnell as history.

Again, when North leads his Pawnees into a Cheyenne village to destroy it, a fifteen-year-old boy guarding the camp's horses flees before the scouts to join the defending warriors, as Luther North tells the story, ". . . while the women and children were getting away. There he died like a warrior. No braver man ever lived than that fifteen year old boy" (196). On the one hand, this episode affirms the Norths' code awarding credit for bravery even to the enemy. On the other hand, the code exists in a context of the brutal treatment of women and children and an entire doomed culture. A tomahawked white woman was found outside the village, Grinnell reports, a victim whose relatives Grinnell himself typically hunts down for documentation. In his reporting these Indian wars, however, his stronger emphasis falls upon slaughter of the Cheyennes who, we would say, have been "demonized" and are to be destroyed in the interests of history.

Two Great Scouts ends in an appropriate climax: General McKenzie's attack on the Cheyenne village of Dull Knife in the winter campaign of 1876-77. Not many are killed on either side, but the Cheyenne horses and food are taken, thus fulfilling the orders, however explicit, to starve and humiliate the Plains Indians into surrender, as a sequence involving some murdered miners indicates. Frank North and his Pawnees are decommissioned shortly after, their work done. Grinnell's purpose was to record the heroism of the scouts before it vanished from memory and when one could still reconstitute, step by step, most of the incidents given here in detail. As a chronicle of action, however, the biography is a monument to a certain view of what American history is about.

Perhaps the most obvious instance of Grinnell as a popularizing mythmaker appears in his earlier series of boys' books centered on a privileged city boy, Jack Danvers, learning to be a man in the wilderness. Beginning with *Jack the Young Ranchman* (1899), the series worked through *Jack among the Indians* (1900) to *Jack the Young Trapper* (1907) and *Jack the Young Cowboy* (1913). These are but several of many adventure-filled fictions written for the period's boys—and men. John MacKenzie notes that juvenile adventure literature was the popular reading of late nineteenth-century adults, when learning to be "manly" and self-reliant was the goal of empire-builders and founders of inspirational organizations like the Boy Scouts.

Like most such fiction, Jack's is an initiation story, in which the West brings out his best. In *Jack the Young Ranchman*, the hero, like the young Theodore Roosevelt, grows up pampered but sickly on New York City's East 38th Street. The doctor prescribes "open-air life and vigorous exercise" on an uncle's Western ranch. Once there, Jack rides and hunts and is taught wilderness lore by the foreman, Hugh, who speaks a rough and direct colloquial English. Hugh, who has been a trapper and Indian trader, tells how to hunt wolves and other animals. Jack tracks and kills his "first" antelope and elk, digs out a wolf den, encounters Indians and cowboys. Feeling much better, he takes a wolf cub, Swiftfoot, back with him to the Big City. The male fantasies laid out here range from Hugh, the elder mentor who can teach Jack what true self-respect is, to shooting big game like a real hunter. Grinnell claimed that all the events in these books really happened, but he has woven them together in a narrative that tells us how much he could rely on the conventions of the genre.

Such fantasy reigns in *Jack among the Indians,* in which Jack, returning to his uncle's ranch the year following his first visit, learns yet more about hunting buffalo, gets caught in quicksand,

and, most importantly, "bonds" with a Piegan boy, Joe, who happens to speak excellent English. Together they hunt with bows and arrows and kill a bear, and Jack rescues a Piegan chief's daughter from the river. Finally, he and Joe return gold they have found on the prairie to its original owner, though they divide the income from the investment, a triumph of honesty and capitalism. Jack kills a thieving Assiniboin attempting to steal the camp's horses, counting coup on him like any warrior. Hugh praises him for being "square," that is, "full of pluck" (194). He is made a member of the Piegan tribe and given the name "White Warrior."

The adventures of Jack are important in the Grinnell canon because they represent more explicitly than does his other work the "regeneration through violence" that Richard Slotkin identifies with United States frontier history and the ideal of manhood forged in hunting and warfare. Jack's self-reliance and his moral and physical courage—along with his acceptance by Indians still challenging and independent—appealed to a post-frontier generation wishing to associate "growing up" with a mythicized heroic past. These books are also Grinnell's most sustained storytelling, fiction which he never attempted for adult readers.

V

Grinnell's major contribution as anthropologist remains his account of the Cheyennes, work published after many years of contact and research from 1890 on. It is the culmination of his writing career. The texts form a trilogy which is epical in its coverage of an entire culture with its heroes and rituals, from its prehistoric beginnings to its end in migration and ruin. *By Cheyenne Campfires* (1926) is a volume of Cheyenne tales and myths. *The Fighting Cheyennes* (1915) is the detailed history of the tribe as a warrior nation against other Plains tribes and whites. The two-volume *The Cheyenne Indians* (1923) represents one of the most intensively compiled records of any Indian people. Here Grinnell's great sympathy for Indian life and his eye trained to observe all the details of a heavily ritualized existence continue to suggest that intensity of "presence" found in his best writing.

For all his investment in the Cheyennes over many years, Grinnell never quite gives up his historic terminology; they are still "savage" and "primitive" people who reason differently than do whites (*Cheyenne Indians* 1: vi). He continues to find in "the old time Cheyennes" those "savage virtues" he had always admired: "honesty, trustworthiness, and bravery in the men," and "courage, devotion, and chastity in the women" (*Fighting Cheyennes* x). Grinnell would also have been drawn to study this tribe by what others have also seen as an exceptional Plains society "with a known sense of form and structured institutions," a cohesive, law-enforcing society, as opposed, for instance, to the "formlessness" of Shoshone "law-stuff" and the "violent individualism of the Comanches" (Llewellyn and Hoebel ix). Furthermore, this model world of warrior values still lived for aged informants who could remember pre-Civil War frontier history as well as stories of migration and warfare told to them by warriors older yet: ". . . the former ways of the wild Cheyennes, the old free life of the Western plains" (*Fighting Cheyennes* xi). There is in Grinnell's anthropology an element not present in the work of his contemporaries: a moral and historical subtext that derives from his concept of the frontier mythos.

Although not published first, *By Cheyenne Campfires* is arguably the introduction to the trilogy since its stories and myths refer back to the earlier Pawnee and Blackfoot collections in organization, continuing Grinnell's contention that narrative reveals most about the "Indian mind." Oral accounts tie the present to the past and provide a new generation with models for contemporary exploits, making even the coup tale, that egotistical bit of bragging, like Beowulf's, responsive to a public context. *By Cheyenne Campfires* opens with an explanation, symbolic in two senses, of the medicine arrows and the sacred hat, inspirational objects given the tribe by its two culture heroes. Preserved generation after generation, they constitute, symbolically, an historical "record" of communal belief and individual responsibility (3). Without comment, Grinnell notes that the loss of the sacred arrows to the Pawnees in a battle and the mistreatment of the sacred hat by its guardians are claimed to be the causes of recent Cheyenne misfortune. This sacred history sets the stage for the stories that follow, beginning with the earliest remembered war tales from before 1825 and coming up to late frontier days. These first tales are about individuals, for the most part, and illustrate bravery, foolhardiness, and men's interaction with the supernatural.

Certain of the stories from the distant and near-mythic past describe otherworldly response to human choice. "The White Horse" tells of the loss of a magic "wheel lance" ("hohk tsim"), which is supposed to protect its owner from arrows or bullets—but doesn't. Captured by the enemy Crows, the lance nevertheless returns of itself to its owner, Old Lodge, when he calls it back: "Soon after he began singing, while all were looking toward the east, they saw coming a little whirlwind of dust. Old Lodge dropped his robe and stood in the path of the whirlwind with his hands stretched out. It came toward him and as it passed he reached out his hands and picked out of it the 'hohk tsim'" (8). In "The Speech of the Wolves," warriors continue on their raiding journey, though warned by very verbal coyotes, and one warrior is killed. Dreams, supernatural visitations, and omens provide help or warnings which may or may not come true. As always with Grinnell, he gives in circumstantial detail the step-by-step advance on the enemy or the rituals of calling up spirits, and he does so without deflecting the effect of the tale by any interpretation or editorial commentary.

See, for instance, "Where Medicine Snake Was Pictured," in which such detail goes into both description of the search for the missing warriors and the ritual in which Elk River summons the spirits to help find them (31-34). Usually, these are "historic" events. An account of Big Head coming back to life after being left for dead concludes: "NOTE: Big Head died in 1857. He was several times shot by the soldiers at Fort Kearny, but always recovered" (27). One would like to know more about Big Head's powers.

These extended war-party stories follow a pattern. They usually begin with individuals deciding to set off in revenge or on a horse-stealing foray, with the leader assigned a brief characterization: "Big Head was the chief man of the Fox Soldiers' Society and a noted warrior" (21). The approach to the enemy camp is established as a challenge to the combined skills of physical prowess and deception. This is followed by a vigorous account of every participant's experience in the ensuing battle, often given in quotation by the fighters to suggest authenticity as in "Bear's Foot and Big Foot" (10-13). Again, Grinnell rarely "interferes." Events and characters' explanations for decisions carry their own "reasons" for happening. White Bull kills an enemy chief exactly like that shown him in a dream, attended by appropriate warnings from a coyote and a magpie.

In the succeeding "Tales of Mystery," Grinnell uses more quoted dialogue to carry the narrative, though this does not create more complex characterization. In "The Buffalo Wife," a Cheyenne version of a tale known throughout the Plains, he gives the story twice, as it were, repeating the narrative with different actors as it must have been in the original telling, Indian storytellers being less concerned with repetition as a flaw than are whites. As with earlier collections, the word "mystery" for Grinnell again means the supernatural and its entry into human life, such entry demanding a moral or spiritual response, usually from an individual on a journey away from the camp into strange dream-like territory. In "The Buffalo Wife," because the young unnamed hero loves his wife and child, he pursues them when they vanish. Their tracks turn into those of a buffalo cow and calf, a familiar bit of shape-changing that signals a certain Indian apprehension about the shadings of likeness and difference between animals and mankind. To recover his family, the searcher must show courage and endurance by following them for four days. Warned by his son, who has become a buffalo calf, the father faces the threat of death from his wife's people, the buffalo. His bravery earns their respect. Because his son teaches him some tricky ways of identifying mother and child, he passes an "identity" test and brings them back to his people. He becomes the legendary rescuer of the tribe from the prehistoric flesh-eating buffalo, a familiar topos in Plains lore: "He was a man of great power, and saved the tribe. That was when we first began to live" (93).

This basic plot is then repeated, but the protagonist is now a "Contrary," a tribal member who lives everything "in reverse," even walking or shooting a bow backwards. In this second version, we get an additional shape-changing, an old woman who clings to Contrary's back by day, but turns into a beautiful woman by night. She waits for him in a glowing lodge at the camp's center and claims him for her husband. Grinnell's unnuanced telling contributes to the effect of mystery: "The young man entered the lodge. The girl looked at him as he went through the doorway, and followed him with her eyes until he said to her, 'Hand me my son.' Then she put the baby in his arms" (97). All proceeds naturally, Contrary's usual reversal of action being ignored in the narrative. The lodge vanishes, as in the first "chapter," and Contrary must follow his family back to their buffalo people and win them again. Courage and skill at trickery go together to "tame" the animals, and so in some sense, the animal in mankind, though Grinnell makes no theoretical analysis of human-animal relationships, presenting only the delightful tale itself.

A story like "The Buffalo Woman" shows how Grinnell's style creates a sense of presence. His model, of course, is the European folk or fairy tale. Strange, irrational elements are incorporated into a forward-moving narration laying out the step-by-step inevitability of the conjunction of human and supernatural. Contrary walks directly into the mysterious tepee and says, without explanation or hesitation, "Give me my child," as though the transformation of an ugly old woman into a beautiful if evasive wife were an everyday experience, exactly as with Cinderella or Little Red Riding Hood, who show no surprise at talking animals who know all about them. Hero myths and stories from prehistoric times conclude *By Cheyenne Campfires*, ending with accounts of the Cheyenne trickster, Wihio. These are wonderfully told tales, uncomplicated by scholarly apparatus, though each one connects with folk story archetypes around the world. That the Cheyennes had such a rich imaginative life is important for Grinnell's "scholarly" point.

Probably *The Fighting Cheyennes* is Grinnell's greatest sustained historical writing. The book recounts the tribe's wars from as far before the Civil War as memory permits, until their ultimate defeat and reduction to reservation life after Little Big Horn. To date, the work is surely the most detailed written record of American Indian history as warfare. Grinnell seems to have consulted every account of Plains campaigns before 1915, from the official military reports of battles to the personal stories of participants. This is unusual United States history, furthermore, in that it is told entirely from the Indian point of view, designed, as Grinnell says, to give a side other than that of white historians (x). In structure, the sequence of chapters, each organized around a battle, has a rising narrative rhythm which extends Grinnell's essentially chronicle style layout into thematic meaning. The decline of the Cheyenne nation from migratory warriors into sedentary farmers learning to become a "component and useful part of the population of the country" (435), seems prepared for by the tribe's early history. Its very conditions for mental and physical survival—dependence on a single major food source and an aggressive individual warrior mentality—could only lead to its demise, whatever other elements like belief in magic helpers and possession of inferior firepower might contribute. Read against the context of Grinnell's culturally more-expansive study of the tribe, *The Fighting Cheyennes* provides a fascinating example of what the war historian William Keegan describes as cultural resistance to necessary changes in military tactics, since to accept new kinds of weapons or different formations in battle would mean entirely recasting the culture itself.

Such a view is implicit in Grinnell's organization with its curve of inevitable decline. He opens with the signatory stories of famous Cheyenne warriors, illustrating the "fighting spirit" in which young men were trained, so that "to them fighting was a real joy." And Grinnell makes a parallel with his own career: "Perhaps they regarded their fights somewhat as the big-game hunter of modern times regards his pursuit of dangerous game" (13). In each chapter minute detail stitches the narrative together. Gone entirely are the romantic locutions of his earlier work. In "The Death of Mouse's Road," a war party sets out to take horses from Kiowas and Comanches, traditional raiding sources. In returning with the stolen horses, however, they are pursued, and Mouse's Road becomes the focus of a sequence of heroic gestures in which, his bow broken, he kills a Comanche chief, stands his ground in the subsequent attack, kills a Mexican allied with the enemy, tries to kill a Kiowa named Lone Wolf, and drives his lance through yet another.

"Now the Kiowas and Comanches saw something that they had never seen before—a man who seemed swifter than a horse, more active than a panther, as strong as a bear, and one against whom weapons seemed useless. There were more than a hundred of the Kiowas and Comanches and only one Cheyenne on foot, without arms, but the Kiowas and Comanches began to run away." They offer this hero a horse and saddle to ride off, but he refuses, "signing that they must kill him." Finally they do, but, his head cut off, "Mouse's Road raised himself and sat upright." Everyone flees, thinking they have killed a powerful medicine man. The thrill of this story's re-creation is underlined by its coming from the admiring enemies, "for all the Cheyennes were killed . . . . The Kiowas and Comanches said that Mouse's Road was the bravest man they ever saw or heard of" (15-17).

As the honorific comparisons to horse, panther, and bear suggest, such stories are epic in their form, and together they establish a pattern of revenge, vendettas, recovery of the slain, and honor paid to the brave, a pattern that reminds us of Homer's *Iliad*, another culture's view of warrior virtues and flaws. Grinnell has accumulated an immense number of such stories—expanded coup tales, really—among them one of a Crow who cried and sang outside the Cheyenne camp and led them into a trap, in revenge for the deaths of at least five thousand Crows in a Cheyenne attack, as one commentator claims. Grinnell mildly says this number seems excessive; this defeat of the Crows "was sufficiently severe without enlargement" (28-30). But the use of the hyperbole is again Homeric.

The first half of *The Fighting Cheyennes* concentrates on wars with other Plains tribes. Grinnell uses careful accumulation of detail—how many horses taken, how a man is given a new name for a victory, in what parts of the body he was wounded—with as much dialogue from participant warrior "historians" as possible. The chapters' progression suggests the ceremonial process of preparing for warfare; the method of selecting men to serve as scouts is an example (84-86), as is a yet more protracted set of rituals later in the text in which Spotted Wolf, "one of the bravest of the old time warriors," shares his protective powers with his son, White Shield, who is about to ride against the United States Army. Grinnell presents the account in dialogue, Spotted Wolf explaining the importance of his son's wearing on certain parts of his costume symbolic figures of a swallow or a kingfisher. This technique shows the reader rather than just describes "the Indian point of view and explains to some extent the Cheyenne belief in the help received from animals" (337-39).

The second half of the book then takes up the Cheyennes' resistance to the whites, Grinnell noting that the Plains tribes were not initially hostile, but suggesting that the massive killing-off of game, the introduction of whiskey, the increase in passage through Indian territory, and the building of forts and towns made life increasingly hard for the native people. Grinnell is as impartial as he can be, using information from both sides where possible. "Additional white testimony" proves that Lt. Earye, leader of the military attack on the Cheyennes at Sand Creek, had attacked the Indians first in an earlier engagement (145-46). The Indians, on the other hand, are represented as "setting out to clear the Platte and Arkansas roads of whites, and terrible work they made of it" (148-51). And he can turn to a description of the unprovoked attack on Black Kettle's camp, a description provided by his old friend George Bent, who lived there with his Cheyenne wife. Bent's story of the attack concludes this chapter, the passage itself ending with the quotation from Colonel Chivington's men that all Indians, "little and big," were to be killed (180), quiet editorial commentary in itself.

The longest chapter is given to a detailed account of the Sand Creek "massacre" and how it led to the Sioux-Cheyenne attack on Fort Kearny (the Fetterman fight) and the battle on the Little Big

Horn with Custer's troops. The history of treaties, signed and broken, the retreat of the Cheyennes deeper into their diminishing territory—all provide a context for the Indians' presentation of their own stories, like that of White Shield: an account of bravery in the face of flight, starvation, and cultural disintegration. Many of the Cheyennes who remained after their final defeat became scouts for the army against other hunted tribes, a grim inversion of their former freedom. Here, where Grinnell's commentary might be condemnatory or ironic, it is only benign: "Almost everyone enjoys hunting, but the hunting of men, when hunted and hunter are equally acute, watchful, and brave, possesses peculiar attractions" (428). The book ends with a brief description of poverty and despair on the Cheyennes' reservations (435), low-keyed in tone compared to impassioned pleas for help from Indian advocates. Grinnell does make such pleas himself, and his specific exposure of corruption in handling affairs on the Blackfeet reservation may have saved that tribe from extinction. As a historian, however, he is careful to preserve what he must have considered a classical calmness of tone.

In some sense, with the two "earlier" books' themes of warfare, hunting, and the powerful mythic weight these activities had in Cheyenne culture, they provide an appropriate introduction and context for Grinnell's major two-volume study of the tribe as a complexly organized Stone Age society contributing to the myth of the western frontier. When the anthropologist Ruth Bunzel praises Grinnell as a "talented amateur," she is disparaging, however lightly, research not based in theoretical or "scientific" training. However, when she picks up on the power of Grinnell's evocation of that lost world—"one can smell the buffalo grass and the wood fires, feel the heavy dew on the prairie" (*Golden Age of Anthropology* 112)—she is in effect praising the immediacy of a descriptive anthropology developed from Grinnell's personal experience as hunter, explorer, and professional writer.

Grinnell might argue that this kind of "contact" anthropology, with its narrative formulation, its wealth of accumulated detail, and its conscientious avoidance of theory and interpretation, is preferable to more "scientific" approaches. It avoids treating its informants as "objects" for study, respecting them appropriately as human beings who have participated with whites in the larger narrative: that of the Western frontier and its restructuring as myth. In his introduction to *The Cheyenne Indians*, Grinnell writes that he has "never been able to regard the Indian as a mere object for study—a museum specimen. . . . While their culture differs from ours in some respects, fundamentally they are like ourselves, except in so far as their environment has obliged them to adopt a mode of life and of reasoning that is not quite our own, and which, without experience, we do not readily understand" (1: vi). "Rubbing shoulders" with Indians—literal "contact"—is the only true justification for recording their way of life. He would certainly be resistant to any suggestion from late twentieth-century critics of anthropology that his methods represented any kind of cultural imperialism.

Given the stories, myths, and biography of Grinnell's earlier works, with their themes of heroic struggle or individual disruption of customary order, we can see why Grinnell organized his study of the Cheyennes to emphasize the importance of habitual actions, of carefully preserved rituals for "coping" with the irrational passion or the extravagantly excessive heroic action. "In the ordinary life of the camp there is much of custom and ceremony . . . a good part of the life of home and camp was conducted after established forms which were supposed to be known to everyone, and the failure to observe these conventions was formerly regarded by Indians as an extraordinary proceeding, much, in fact, as a breach of good manners would be looked at by well-reared people in civilized society" (Brown 176). One could also argue, however, that it was this intensely lived code of conduct that gave Cheyenne life its deepest values and also kept them from changing, from adapting new defenses against their coming destruction.

The first volume of *The Cheyenne Indians* opens with chapters on the tribe's pre-history: their migrations, their "old-time ways" of costume, transportation, hunting with bow and arrows. The narrative beginning, however, is the third chapter, "Village Life," in which Grinnell imagines the incidents of a camp day before white contact: hunters returning with meat, women preparing it or hides and skins, or gambling, young men roaming the camp flirting with the carefully reserved girls. These are all details of a purposive and accustomed order of activities. And somewhere in the text there will be a description of each activity so detailed that it could be duplicated today, should one have a buffalo hide to cure or arrows to make.

The imagined vision of "village life," with its encompassing context for all technical accounts that follow, is still cast in a romantic light, one this fabrication of an Indian "scene" probably can never avoid. Here is nightfall: ". . . the barking of dogs, the yelp of some sportive boy, the shout of some old man calling a friend to a feast, the musical laughter of the women, and in the distance the shrill howl of coyotes; one by one the fires burn down, and at last the camp was as silent as the prairie had been before the people moved in" (1: 70). The chapter's idyll concludes, however, with an account of Buffalo Wallow Woman. As a girl, she daringly tried to ride an unbroken colt through the camp after everyone was asleep, but the colt tossed her off and threw the camp into confusion. Grinnell uses this small moment of theater to conclude the scene with humor.

Wherever he can, Grinnell inserts the story (taken from the informant) of an individual like Buffalo Wallow Woman to illustrate the operation of ceremony or custom. In his chapter on social organization and the importance of clans and less formal associations, he explains the name of a group derived from its leader, Buffalo Chief. This was a man who had killed members of his own tribe, a terrible action. His followers thereafter kept apart, ashamed. The effects of breaking a taboo are shown in the group's historical drama (1: 98-100).

Grinnell explains in detail the training of boys and girls, with the proviso that, though the Cheyennes "were savages of the stone age, their code of sexual morality was that held by the most civilized peoples . . ." (1: 103). And he expresses certain preferences of his own in praising children's training based not on some abstract definition of heaven or hell but on the child's place in the tribal community, a status earned by winning "respect and approbation." Numerous individuals' stories reveal the success—or failure—of such an education, here and in the chapter significantly titled "Woman and Her Place." There were more cases of sexual conflict, of course, than the standard anthropologist's analysis might suggest.

Establishing the sense of presence, of "being there," is still Grinnell's goal. In "Industries," he describes the step-by-step construction of a special ceremonial lodge, down to the specific people who may walk over the hides being prepared on the ground and those who may not. For the lodge's initiation only a man who had killed an enemy in the enemy's own tepee could sanctify it by striking the doorway, telling his coup tale, and entering the lodge first. In historical times, Grinnell saw Little Bear perform this ceremony, illustrating that narrative continuity the anthropologist believes important (1: 231-32).

The second volume of *The Cheyenne Indians* divides into four sections: discussion of warfare and its rituals; the Cheyenne religion, with its correlaries of healing illness and fear of death; and a long account of the principle ceremonies of the tribe, involving the Medicine Lodge and the Massaum ceremony. The "Medicine Lodge" is the familiar Plains sun dance, and Grinnell uses his own witnessing of one given in his time as basis for his report, telling everything that must be said and done, from the detail of an initiate's instructor smoothing the ground with his right thumb, to the sequence of events in the closing moments (2: 211-84). The fourth section is the story of "Sweet Medicine," the culture hero who brought the sacred arrows to the Cheyennes, ending with his prophecy placing the tribe's decline into present time from mythic: People will come who "will ask you for your flesh, . . . but you must say 'no.' They will try to teach you their way of living. If you give up to them your flesh (your children), those that they take away will never know anything. They will work with their hands. They will tear up the earth, and at last you will do it with them. When you do, you will become crazy, and will forget all that I am now teaching you" (2: 381). Apocalyptic visions tend to be self-evident in their consequences, and this one is no exception.

Grinnell's "trilogy" on the Cheyennes gives a more detailed representation of a Plains Indian culture than nearly any other. Only a book-length study of the language is missing. The fact that this "contact" anthropology derives not from laboratory or classroom scholarship but from the white man's equivalent of a hunting warrior culture, is a nineteenth-century European-American phenomenon. Paradoxically, what made this kind of ethnology possible was the establishment of an American empire based on the frontier mythos. Even as Grinnell collected and wrote, he knew Indian culture was being destroyed; he uses the term "vanishing" in a kind of double-think typical of his period. His vision is inevitably a tragic one, and he is to be honored for the cultural dignity which his narratives award the Pawnees or the Cheyennes, an approach not always available to his contemporary scholars digging up graves for bones and museum artifacts. He is also to be thanked for the development of a writing style in which he tried to represent the Indian less as a sentimentalized stereotype and more as an individual telling the story of his culture through his own voice.

Of course a certain distortion is still there, inevitable in history rendered in translation and through Grinnell's narrative and ideological preferences. But we can see what he avoids in his approach by looking at the photographs used to illustrate *The Cheyenne Indians* or *By Cheyenne Campfires* with their falsely posed Indian models. Working within the framework of a wilderness frontier ending even as it reached its fulfillment, Grinnell has left us its history perhaps only his kind of personal experience could provide.

Grinnell is an important figure in Western American literature who has been left out of the spotlight as a writer paradoxically because of his accomplishments. In recording and preserving oral tales and myths and the cultural history of American Indian tribes, he wrote books that have been classified as "anthropology," a social science concerned with the gathering of information and with cultural interpretation. Grinnell's passion for detail, for authentic self-representation by native informants, his consistent interest in locating each "artifact" within its appropriate tribal site, and his resistance to developing theories about native life as the basis for analysis of a culture, would seem to put him in the category of the collection-forming "bone hunter," as so many early anthropologists were.

What Grinnell's major works reveal, however, is his power as a writer of narrative whose effort to describe "presence" with exactly these anthropological ingredients ensures for a modern reader the imaginative recovery of those mythic or historic lives. Contemporary study of native peoples and their cultures depends heavily not only upon "contact" anthropology (that is, personal involvement in day-by-day events) but also upon representing a society's life as a narratival structure with a beginning, an ending, and plotted experiences in between. Grinnell's important books are in print not only because of present scholarly interest in the American West and its peoples but also because of his early commitment to "story-telling," to narrative representation of those frontier lives, that goes beyond just bone hunting.

Selected Bibliography

PRIMARY SOURCES

BOOKS BY GEORGE BIRD GRINNELL

American Big Game Hunting. Ed. Grinnell and Theodore Roosevelt. New York: Forest and Stream, 1893.

American Big Game in Its Haunts. Ed. Grinnell. New York: Forest and Stream, 1904.

American Game Bird Shooting. New York: Forest and Stream, 1910.

Blackfoot Indian Stories. New York: Scribner's, 1914.

Blackfoot Lodge Tales: The Story of a Prairie People. 1892. Lincoln: U of Nebraska P, 1962.

By Cheyenne Campfires. 1926. New Haven: Yale UP, 1962.

The Cheyenne Indians: Their History and Ways of Life. 1923. 2 vols. New York: Cooper Square, 1962.

The Fighting Cheyennes. 1915. Norman: U of Oklahoma P, 1956.

The Indians of Today. 1900. New York: Duffield, 1911.

Pawnee Hero Stories and Folk Tales; With Notes on the Origins, Customs and Character of the Pawnee People. 1889. Lincoln: U of Nebraska P, 1961.

The Punishment of the Stingy and Other Indian Stories. 1901. Lincoln: U of Nebraska P, 1982.

The Story of the Indian. New York: D. Appleton, 1895.

Two Great Scouts and Their Pawnee Battalion. Cleveland: Arthur H. Clark, 1928.

When Buffalo Ran. 1920. Norman: U of Oklahoma P, 1966.

JACK DANVERS SERIES
Jack the Young Ranchman. 1899.
Jack among the Indians. 1900.
Jack in the Rockies. 1904.
Jack the Young Canoeman. 1906.
Jack the Young Trapper. 1907.
Jack the Young Explorer. 1908.
Jack the Young Cowboy. 1913.

SECONDARY SOURCES

Brown, Dee, ed. *Pawnee, Blackfoot and Cheyenne: History and Folklore of the Plains from the Writings of George Bird Grinnell.* New York: Scribner's, 1961.

Diettert, Gerald. *Grinnell's Glacier: George Bird Grinnell and Glacier National Park.* Missoula: Mountain Press, 1992.

Ewers, John C. *The Blackfeet: Raiders on the Northwestern Plains.* Norman: U of Oklahoma P, 1958.

Hoebel, Adamson. *The Cheyennes: Indians of the Great Plains.* New York: Holt, 1960.

Lears, Jackson. *No Place of Grace.* New York: Pantheon, 1981.

Lewellyn, K. N., and E. Adamson Hoebel. *The Cheyenne Way: Conflict and Case Law in Primitive Jurisprudence.* Norman: U of Oklahoma P, 1941.

Levin, David. *History as Romantic Art.* Stanford: Stanford UP, 1959.

Mead, Margaret, and Ruth L. Bunzel, eds. *The Golden Age of American Anthropology.* New York: Braziller, 1960.

Mitchell, Lee Clark. *Witness to a Vanishing America: The Nineteenth-Century Response.* Princeton: Princeton UP, 1981.

Muir, John. *Travels in Alaska.* Boston: Houghton Mifflin, 1916.

Reiger, John F., ed. *The Passing of the Great West: Selected Papers of George Bird Grinnell.* New York: Winchester, 1972.

Roosevelt, Theodore. *Ranch Life and the Hunting Trail*. New York: Century, 1888.

Slotkin, Richard. *The Fatal Environment: The Myth of the Frontier in the Age of Industrialization, 1800-1890*. New York: Atheneum, 1985.

Trefethen, James B. *An American Crusade for Wildlife*. New York: Winchester, 1975.

White, G. Edward. *The Eastern Establishment and the Western Experience*. New Haven: Yale UP, 1968.